Acting Edition

Thespy Playwriting 2021

The Plant Crusade
by Aubrey Luse

Oakland
by Bridget Phillips

Reverie
by Jacqueline Vellandi

The Plant Crusade Copyright © 2022 by Aubrey Luse
Oakland Copyright © 2022 by Bridget Phillips
Reverie Copyright © 2022 by Jacqueline Vellandi
All Rights Reserved

THESPY PLAYWRITING 2021 is fully protected under the copyright laws of the United States of America, the British Commonwealth, including Canada, and all member countries of the Berne Convention for the Protection of Literary and Artistic Works, the Universal Copyright Convention, and/or the World Trade Organization conforming to the Agreement on Trade Related Aspects of Intellectual Property Rights. All rights, including professional and amateur stage productions, recitation, lecturing, public reading, motion picture, radio broadcasting, television, online/digital production, and the rights of translation into foreign languages are strictly reserved.

ISBN 978-0-573-70954-8

www.concordtheatricals.com
www.concordtheatricals.co.uk

FOR PRODUCTION INQUIRIES

UNITED STATES AND CANADA
info@concordtheatricals.com
1-866-979-0447

UNITED KINGDOM AND EUROPE
licensing@concordtheatricals.co.uk
020-7054-7298

Each title is subject to availability from Concord Theatricals Corp., depending upon country of performance. Please be aware that *THESPY PLAYWRITING 2021* may not be licensed by Concord Theatricals Corp. in your territory. Professional and amateur producers should contact the nearest Concord Theatricals Corp. office or licensing partner to verify availability.

CAUTION: Professional and amateur producers are hereby warned that *THESPY PLAYWRITING 2021* is subject to a licensing fee. The purchase, renting, lending or use of this book does not constitute a license to perform this title(s), which license must be obtained from Concord Theatricals Corp. prior to any performance. Performance of this title(s) without a license is a violation of federal law and may subject the producer and/or presenter of such performances to civil penalties. Both amateurs and professionals considering a production are strongly advised to apply to the appropriate agent before starting rehearsals, advertising, or booking a theatre. A licensing fee must be paid whether the title(s) is presented for charity or gain and whether or not admission is charged. Professional/Stock licensing fees are quoted upon application to Concord Theatricals Corp.

This work is published by Samuel French, an imprint of Concord Theatricals Corp.

No one shall make any changes in this title(s) for the purpose of production. No part of this book may be reproduced, stored in a retrieval system, scanned, uploaded, or transmitted in any form, by any means, now known or yet to be invented, including mechanical, electronic, digital, photocopying, recording, videotaping, or otherwise, without the prior written permission of the publisher. No one shall share this title(s), or any part of this title(s), through any social media or file hosting websites.

For all inquiries regarding motion picture, television, online/digital and other media rights, please contact Concord Theatricals Corp.

MUSIC AND THIRD-PARTY MATERIALS USE NOTE

Licensees are solely responsible for obtaining formal written permission from copyright owners to use copyrighted music and/or other copyrighted third-party materials (e.g., artworks, logos) in the performance of this play and are strongly cautioned to do so. If no such permission is obtained by the licensee, then the licensee must use only original music and materials that the licensee owns and controls. Licensees are solely responsible and liable for clearances of all third-party copyrighted materials, including without limitation music, and shall indemnify the copyright owners of the play(s) and their licensing agent, Concord Theatricals Corp., against any costs, expenses, losses and liabilities arising from the use of such copyrighted third-party materials by licensees. For music, please contact the appropriate music licensing authority in your territory for the rights to any incidental music.

IMPORTANT BILLING AND CREDIT REQUIREMENTS

If you have obtained performance rights to this title, please refer to your licensing agreement for important billing and credit requirements.

ABOUT THESPY PLAYWRITING

Thespy Playwriting is part of the International Thespian Excellence Awards (Thespys) and is a writing contest and script development program for high school students, sponsored by the Educational Theatre Association. Each year, up to four finalists are invited to the International Thespian Festival, where the students work with a professional director, a dramaturg, and a volunteer cast of actors to put their short plays on their feet before a live audience.

Originally launched in 1994 under the name "Playworks," the program aims to nurture young playwrights. Over its history, many participants have gone on to college majors and careers in theatre, writing, and related fields. Whatever the eventual future of the writers or their scripts, Thespy Playwriting is an exhilarating experience in a creative discipline seldom taught in schools or celebrated in the wider culture.

Students qualify in the Playwriting category of the Thespys throughout the year by earning a Superior rating at a local qualifying event. The qualifying students then advance to the international round, where up to four of the top scoring student playwrights are selected to workshop their pieces, culminating in a live reading. Each play is reviewed by three adjudicators at the local level, then by three more adjudicators at the international level. All applicants receive detailed scores and educational feedback at each level to promote their growth as a writer.

For more information about Thespy Playwriting, please visit https://thespys.org.

CONTENTS

The Plant Crusade..1
Oakland... 23
Reverie... 37

THE PLANT CRUSADE

Aubrey Luse

THE PLANT CRUSADE was first produced by Redmond Proficiency Academy and the International Thespian Festival over Zoom on June 25th, 2021. The performance was directed by Stewart Hawk, with dramaturgical work by Nicholas Pappas. The production stage manager was Jamie Ko. The cast was as follows:

OPHELIA	London Griffin
KIMBERLY	Spencer Wareing
CARTER	Seth Gunawardena
BROCK	Aubrey Luse
VIVIENNE	Bella Borgart
MS. WILSON	Alison Avery

CHARACTERS

OPHELIA
KIMBERLY
CARTER
BROCK
VIVIENNE
MS. WILSON

SETTING

A high school, located in a homophobic area of America.

TIME

Anywhere from 1980 to present day.

AUTHOR'S NOTES

There is no music mentioned in this show, but it can be added at the director's discretion. Ideally, the inclusion of music would be music in the style of recognizable pop from the chosen time period, played during scene transitions. A license to produce *The Plant Crusade* does not include a performance license for any third-party or copyrighted music. Licensees should create an original composition or use music in the public domain. For further information, please see the Music and Third Party Materials Use Note on page iii.

Scene One: Locker Room

(OPHELIA stands in a spotlight, reading from a magnetic word board. Her voice echoes, almost dreamlike, as she reads a poem.)

OPHELIA. Calm is a miracle, / I am a wreck. / Freedom is sickness, / I am immune. / My humanity is a cage.

KIMBERLY. *(Suddenly.)* Ophelia. Ophelia! Come on, I was just getting to the good part.

(The lights come up, and we see OPHELIA in the girls' locker room, still staring at the board. Other students mill about, finishing the process of changing out of their gym clothes. KIMBERLY gets done tying her shoes, and continues talking.)

Are you even listening to me?

OPHELIA. *(Distracted.)* Uh huh, totally.

(KIMBERLY sighs and walks over to OPHELIA. This is clearly not an uncommon occurrence.)

KIMBERLY. Alright, fine, we'll do your thing. What're you looking at?

OPHELIA. *(Finally snapping back to reality.)* Hmm? Oh, sorry Kim, there's just this weird poem on the magnet board, I got a bit distracted.

KIMBERLY. Wait, someone really went for Ms. Wilson's team-building activity? God, how much time do you have to have on your hands in order to write magnet poetry between classes?

OPHELIA. That's – I mean, sure, I guess you're right, but that's not the point. It's actually a pretty good poem. Someone really poured their heart into it.

> (**KIMBERLY** *scans the poem, and then quickly dismisses it.*)

KIMBERLY. Yeah, sure, whatever. Come on, we're gonna be late for lunch, you know how fast they run out of tater tots.

OPHELIA. You go on ahead, I'll catch up in a minute.

KIMBERLY. *(Confused.)* Why?

OPHELIA. Oh, I uh… I just gotta ask Ms. Wilson something

KIMBERLY. Okay, whatever.

> (**KIMBERLY** *shrugs and leaves.* **OPHELIA** *looks around at the mostly empty locker room, and then starts rearranging the magnets. Once she's satisfied, she takes a step back, and reads it aloud.*)

OPHELIA. I sacrifice sickness / I cut tension and skip emergency / We are the plant crusade / We grow

Scene Two: Cafeteria

> (**OPHELIA** *walks in with her lunch and sits down at the table with* **KIMBERLY** *and* **CARTER**, *who are oblivious to all their surroundings. Other students populate the rest of the lunchroom.*)

KIMBERLY. *(Offended.)* Babe, how could you say something like that! I can't believe you!

CARTER. I'm sorry, Kimmy, but it's just the truth. I love you more.

KIMBERLY. No! I love YOU more!

CARTER. No, I love you more!

KIMBERLY. No –

> (*They are interrupted by* **OPHELIA** *loudly clearing her throat.*)

Oh, there you are Ophelia! You can settle our argument: Who loves the other more?

OPHELIA. Isn't that kind of...arbitrary?

KIMBERLY. *(Groaning.)* Ophelia...

CARTER. Babe, she already knows the truth. I love you the most. I can't wait for you to come over tonight, my parents won't be home so we can totally –

OPHELIA. Well, would you look at the time! Nice to see you, Carter, but I just remembered I... *(She tries to come up with an excuse, and fails.)* don't...want to be here...anymore.

> (*She laughs nervously, and gets up from the table.*)

KIMBERLY. Wait, Ophelia, stay, we wanna hang out with you! God, why do you always leave when Carter gets here?

CARTER. Come on Kim, isn't it obvious? Ophelia's...well, you know.

OPHELIA. *(Suddenly turning quite defensive.)* What, Carter? What's obvious?

CARTER. Come on, everyone sees how you look at Kim. Face it, you're totally a lesbian.

OPHELIA. Okay, that is completely ridiculous. Even if I was gay, which I'm NOT, I would never go for Kim. I mean, no offense Kim, you're just not my type.

(Beat.)

Because you're a girl! And girls aren't my type. I'm totally straight!

CARTER. Come on Ophelia, it's hot. If you and Kimmy wanna go make out, that's cool with me. As long as I get to watch, of course.

*(**OPHELIA** is beet red and utterly speechless. **KIMBERLY** is scandalized, and not happy about being dragged into this.)*

KIMBERLY. Carter!

CARTER. What? It's true!

KIMBERLY. I cannot even begin to describe everything that's wrong with what you just said. You can't just go around calling everyone a...a lesbian...when they don't want to be around you. I am NOT into that, and neither is she. I know Ophelia better than anyone, she's totally normal.

*(Their conversation is interrupted by **BROCK** running up to their lunch table, with **VIVIENNE** trailing behind.)*

BROCK. Hey Carter, I've been looking for you! Do you think you could help me work on my throw before practice today?

CARTER. Yeah, totally!

BROCK. Awesome!

CARTER. You gonna come cheer us on, Viv? We might need a little motivation, if you know what I mean.

> (**KIMBERLY** *looks shocked, and she slaps* **CARTER** *on the arm.* **VIVIENNE** *rolls her eyes.*)

VIVIENNE. Gross. I see why no one but your girlfriend wants to hang out with you. Aside from, you know,

> (*She gestures vaguely to the entirety of* **CARTER**, *who frowns.*)

the obvious.

OPHELIA. Sorry, Vivienne, Carter's incapable of making a decision that doesn't involve his crotch.

> (**VIVIENNE** *looks* **KIMBERLY** *up and down, unimpressed.*)

VIVIENNE. Clearly. I'll see you later, Brock.

BROCK. See ya!

> (**VIVIENNE** *walks away.* **OPHELIA, KIMBERLY,** *and* **CARTER** *all look offended, but* **BROCK** *has not noticed anything amiss.*)

Man, isn't Viv great?

> (*The others make vague, noncommittal noise.*)

CARTER. If we're going to practice, Brock, we should do it now. Mr. Johnson will kill me if I'm late to class again.

BROCK. Hah. Johnson.

> (**BROCK** *and* **CARTER** *exit, leaving the girls alone.* **OPHELIA** *tries to talk to a still-fuming* **KIMBERLY.**)

OPHELIA. So Kim. About what Carter said –

KIMBERLY. Who does Vivienne think she is?? I can't believe she got Carter to flirt with her right in front of me. She claims she's "waiting until marriage," but there's just no way. I bet she's banged half the guys in the school by now. Lord knows anyone who dresses like that is just asking for it.

OPHELIA. No, actually, um, I meant the...lesbian thing.

KIMBERLY. Oh right! God, he's such a dumbass. Don't worry, he doesn't actually think that about you, he's just a perv. He's lucky he's so hot.

OPHELIA. *(Visibly relieved.)* Okay, good.

KIMBERLY. Yeah, don't worry about it, Ophelia. We both know you're...you know.

OPHELIA. Right. Totally normal.

Scene Three: Locker Room

(The next day, students are getting ready for gym in the locker room. **OPHELIA** *is among them, and she steps over to the magnet board.* **MS. WILSON** *notices her, and walks over.)*

MS. WILSON. Oh no, Ophelia, that was your poem, wasn't it? Sorry about that, I think one of the period one girls messed it up. They use that thing to make dirty jokes like their lives depend on it. Honestly, it's almost impressive at this point.

OPHELIA. No, uh... I think this is a response, actually? They left the last line of my poem, but they added this. *(She begins to read.)* My throat is tight. / Sickness, cigarettes, cancer. / To grow is a sacrifice. / I will not dare to be difficult.

(They sit with the poem for a beat.)

Ms. Wilson, do you know who wrote this?

MS. WILSON. *(She thinks for a moment.)* Sorry, I have no idea. It's gotta be someone from first period, your poem was still there when we started cheer practice yesterday. But beyond that, I've got nothing.

OPHELIA. That's alright, I'm sure I can figure it out.

MS. WILSON. I have no doubt about that. Oh, and make sure you write something back! You don't want to keep her waiting.

*(***MS. WILSON*** walks away.)*

OPHELIA. Right. *(She spends a moment rearranging magnets.)* Is this eternal? / We yearn / We demand pleasant tension / You inspire me / But you wreck me / Dare I guess?

Scene Four: Cafeteria

(It is a few weeks later, and **OPHELIA**, **KIMBERLY**, *and* **CARTER** *are all eating lunch together, in the middle of a conversation. Other students populate the lunchroom as well, including* **BROCK**, *who is sitting at a table nearby.)*

CARTER. So let me get this straight: you've been trading poems back and forth in the locker room for two weeks now, and you still have no idea who it is you're writing to?

KIMBERLY. I can't believe you've been keeping this from me for so long.

OPHELIA. To be fair, you have the shortest attention span known to man. I can't remember the last time I actually heard the end of one of your stories.

KIMBERLY. That's because you're never listening. But never mind all that, you need to come over to my house tonight, we can try to figure out who this chick is. If your poem is always there after school, then it's gotta be one of the first period girls. This'll be a piece of cake.

CARTER. But Kimmy, you need to come to the game tonight! You're my good luck charm, I can't score the winning touchdown if you're not cheering me on from the stands.

KIMBERLY. Oh yeah! Ophelia, you gotta come to the game with us. It's going to be a blast.

OPHELIA. I don't know, I have a lot of homework I need to catch up on, and I don't really do well with crowds...

KIMBERLY. Ugh, don't be a buzzkill. It'll be fun! *(Suggestively.)* Brock will be there, too. He's totally into you, you know.

CARTER. Wait, I thought Brock was banging Vivienne.

KIMBERLY. No, I think all Vivienne cares about is getting attention from as many guys as physically possible. Besides, Brock was making googly eyes at Ophelia all day in English.

*(She notices **BROCK** sitting at another table.)*

In fact, I think he's making googly eyes at you right now.

*(**KIMBERLY** motions **BROCK** over, and he sits down with the rest of them.)*

What's up Brock? Something on your mind?

BROCK. Um, yeah, actually. Can I ask you a question, Ophelia?

OPHELIA. Uh, sure.

BROCK. Well, the thing is, you're the smartest girl I know. And I'm kind of nervous to ask, but it's gone on too long now, and I just need to know. What kind of animal is the Pink Panther?

OPHELIA. It's...it's a panther, Brock.

BROCK. Well, I know that, I'm not stupid. But like, is it a lion? I don't think it's a tiger, because tigers have stripes, but they're also not usually pink, so I'm just not sure.

OPHELIA. *(Turning back to **KIMBERLY**.)* Googly eyes. Right.

KIMBERLY. Ugh, fine. Whatever. But please still come with us?

OPHELIA. *(Sighing.)* I mean, I didn't have time to write a poem today, and I might miss the bus if I try to write one after school, so... Alright. Fine.

KIMBERLY. Yes! We're gonna have SO much fun. Carter is the best at football.

CARTER. Well, I mean, they don't make you the team captain for nothing.

BROCK. ...you guys are useless. I'll go ask Viv.

KIMBERLY. Careful, Brock, she's venomous.

Scene Five: Locker Room

(OPHELIA walks into the locker room, and almost bumps right into MS. WILSON. It's after school, and the locker room is deserted.)

MS. WILSON. Oh, sorry Ophelia! I hate to be a party pooper, but you're not technically supposed to be here while a game's going on, we gotta keep all the kids in the same place or it becomes a safety issue.

OPHELIA. *(Verging on frantic.)* I know, and I'm sorry, but I didn't have time to write a new poem today, and –

MS. WILSON. Hey, hey, calm down. It's alright, I'm not mad, you can go do your thing. Just, try to remember next time, okay?

OPHELIA. Yes, okay, thank you so much!

MS. WILSON. You're welcome. Hurry back when you're done.

OPHELIA. Will do!

(OPHELIA walks further into the locker room, and starts rearranging words on the magnet board. She hears the other door to the locker room swing open, and she snaps to attention, but it's too late. VIVIENNE has already noticed her.)

VIVIENNE. Wh – what are you doing?

OPHELIA. Nothing, Vivienne! I mean, not NOTHING nothing, technically it would be physically impossible to do nothing, but –

VIVIENNE. Cut the crap, Ophelia.

OPHELIA. Okay, fine, I was just – I write poems here, every day, and it's just kind of a writing exercise I do, and I have a friend that writes me back sometimes, and –

VIVIENNE. *(She gets it; her eyes go wide.)* Oh god.

OPHELIA. Listen, I know it's kinda corny, but it's fun, and my writing skills have gotten a lot better because of it, just, there's really no need to make fun of me, okay?

VIVIENNE. Wait, no, shut up for a second. YOU'RE the one who's been writing to me?

OPHELIA. Wh...writing to YOU?

(Both girls stare at each other for a second.)

No, it...it can't be you, you're not in first period gym!

VIVIENNE. Um, no, why does that matter?

OPHELIA. Because I have gym during third period, and the poem is still there at the end of the day, and since Ms. Wilson doesn't have a second period class, first period is the only time the poem could have been changed!

VIVIENNE. Not if it gets changed during cheer practice.

OPHELIA. ...Oh.

(Both girls open their mouths to say something, and this is the exact moment that **MS. WILSON** *walks back into the main room.)*

MS. WILSON. Oh, hey Viv, aren't you supposed to be out cheering with the other ladies? And Ophelia, I thought you were just coming in here to finish your poem.

VIVIENNE. *(Obviously lying.)* Actually, Ms. Wilson, I hurt...my... Ankle! Yep, I hurt my ankle. And Ophelia here was kind enough to...help me. With my hurt ankle. So everything's good and fine and you don't need to be here.

MS. WILSON. Oh, if you hurt your ankle, you should've just told me. Ophelia doesn't need to be stuck with helping, that's a teacher's job.

VIVIENNE. She's actually a...junior lifeguard, so she's very experienced.

MS. WILSON. But still –

OPHELIA. Actually, you know what, Vivienne's right, I need help. Could you run and get her some ice?

MS. WILSON. Right, yep, ice. I'll be a minute, are you ladies okay down here by yourselves?

OPHELIA & VIVIENNE. *(Simultaneously.)* YEP!

MS. WILSON. Okay, I'll be right back.

>   (**MS. WILSON** *leaves. The girls look at each other for a moment, before bursting into laughter.*)

VIVIENNE. You're really smart, you know that?

OPHELIA. Oh! Um, thank you.

>   (*The girls both end up looking at the magnet board, poem half-finished.* **VIVIENNE** *finally breaks the silence.*)

VIVIENNE. So...it really is you, then.

OPHELIA. Yeah. I'm sorry if I'm not quite what you expected.

VIVIENNE. No, no, don't apologize, it's just...

OPHELIA. Just what?

VIVIENNE. *(Suddenly self-conscious.)* Never mind, this is stupid, I should get back to the game –

>   (*She moves to stand up, but* **OPHELIA** *grabs her wrist.*)

OPHELIA. No, it's...please, stay.

>   (**VIVIENNE** *sits back down.* **OPHELIA** *reluctantly lets go.*)

VIVIENNE. It's just that...part of me wished it wasn't real. I wanted to believe that I had made it all up somehow. Because...

OPHELIA. Because you were scared. You were scared of the power that...that I could hold over you. God, Vivienne, that's...

VIVIENNE. Shut up, okay, I know it's dumb, you don't need to rub it in.

OPHELIA. No, I was going to say it was sweet.

VIVIENNE. Oh.

OPHELIA. Look, I don't know what kind of friends you have, but I'm not going to be mean to you for no reason. I'm not going to act like –

VIVIENNE. Like me.

(Beat.)

I'm...so sorry, Ophelia.

OPHELIA. You act like that because you're used to people betraying you, aren't you? You're rude to people you hardly know because you don't want to give them the chance to hurt you.

VIVIENNE. *(Dryly.)* My poems told you that much, huh?

OPHELIA. Oh no, Vivienne, I'm sorry, I didn't mean to overstep, I was just guessing –

VIVIENNE. Ophelia, stop apologizing, you haven't done anything wrong. And you can call me Viv, by the way.

OPHELIA. Okay. Sorr – I mean, thank you, Viv.

*(After a beat, **VIVIENNE** shifts suddenly, looking directly at **OPHELIA**. There is no awkwardness left in the conversation now, only tension remains. The girls lean closer to each other with every passing second.)*

VIVIENNE. Can I ask you something?

OPHELIA. I guess, yeah?

VIVIENNE. Why did you write to me, Ophelia?

OPHELIA. I... Told you, didn't I? I wanted writing practice.

VIVIENNE. ...And?

OPHELIA. ...And I was looking for a friend?

VIVIENNE. A friend? Is that all?

OPHELIA. No.

VIVIENNE. I think I know why you wrote to me.

OPHELIA. You do?

VIVIENNE. Yeah. I think you wanted this. You wanted to find out who I was, and talk to me, and then get closer, and then you'd know if this is really who you are. So I guess the real question is... Is this who you are?

> *(At this point, **VIVIENNE** and **OPHELIA** are so close that they can hardly see anything else. **VIVIENNE** is gently holding on to **OPHELIA**, who is mesmerized by her.)*

OPHELIA. Yes.

> *(Both girls close the gap between them at the same time, and their lips meet. Then just like that, it's over, and both girls stare, holding each other.)*

VIVIENNE. You're gay, aren't you, Ophelia.

OPHELIA. Uh, yeah. I think I am.

> *(Suddenly, **OPHELIA** is very aware of the reality of the situation, and it terrifies her.)*

Oh my god, Viv, please don't tell anybody!

VIVIENNE. Tell them? Yeah, I'm sure that would go over well. "Hey Melissa, Ophelia's totally a lesbian. What, how do I know? Oh, no reason, just that we totally kissed in the girls' locker room."

    (**OPHELIA** *giggles, nerves fading.*)

You won't tell anyone, either, right?

OPHELIA. Viv, I would never.

VIVIENNE. I need more than that. I like you and all, but word gets around fast, and if my dad found out… I need you to promise me that you'll keep this a secret.

OPHELIA. I promise, I won't tell a soul. I've had some experience with secrets, believe me.

    (**OPHELIA** *looks away, and takes a deep, shuddering breath. Tears form in the corner of her eyes, and* **VIVIENNE** *takes notice.*)

VIVIENNE. (*Unbearably soft.*) Whoa, hey, what's wrong? Did I say something?

OPHELIA. No, no, you're wonderful, Viv.

    (*Beat.*)

I don't mean to depress you or anything, but…what's next? Shit, Viv, I'm gay. How do I live like this? How do I wake up every morning and keep being normal?

    (**VIVIENNE** *gently takes* **OPHELIA**'s *face in her hands, and looks her deep in the eyes.*)

VIVIENNE. Listen to me. There is nothing, and I mean nothing, wrong with you. Just because you experience attraction differently, that doesn't mean you're broken. You are amazing, and everything about you is amazing. None of that changes now. If anything, you're more yourself, which just means there's more of you to love.

(VIVIENNE lowers her hands, and takes hold of OPHELIA's.)

I don't know what comes next. I don't know if you want this, or if you want me, and if you want to pretend this never happened, I will absolutely oblige. But I need you to know that this is not your last shot, Ophelia. It gets better. It has to. Somewhere in the future, you'll be doing something mundane with someone you love more than life itself, and you're going to realize that you're okay. We're all going to be okay.

(OPHELIA wipes away the last of her tears, then wraps her arms around VIVIENNE.)

OPHELIA. Thank you, Viv.

(They both lean back from the hug and start to go in for another kiss, but MS. WILSON enters the room suddenly with an ice pack. Embarrassed, the girls jump away from each other, both beet red.)

MS. WILSON. I got the ice!

VIVIENNE. Oh, right, yes, thank you.

MS. WILSON. The game's almost over, Ophelia, you should head back out there if you don't want to miss the ending.

OPHELIA. Is that alright with you, Vivienne?

VIVIENNE. Of course. I'll see you later.

(OPHELIA starts to leave, then she realizes that she forgot something.)

OPHELIA. Oh! I almost forgot.

(She walks over to the magnet board as a spotlight comes up, and everyone else fades

into darkness. She rearranges for a moment, then steps back to read her work.)

I understand the cage / But I think instead, I will love you / For you are my plant crusade, / and we were built to grow.

End of Play

OAKLAND

Bridget Phillips

OAKLAND was first produced at the International Thespian Festival over Zoom on June 25, 2021. The performance was directed by Michael Daehn with dramaturgical work by Judy GeBauer. The production stage manager was Autumn Hendrickson. The cast was as follows:

ISAAC...Joshua Israel
MARGARET...Maggie Weller

CHARACTERS

ISAAC – Black. Sixteen years old.
MARGARET – White. Sixteen years old.

SETTING

Bushrod Park, Oakland.

TIME

2 AM

AUTHOR'S NOTES

Quick, impulsive – aside from pauses, which are long and contemplative.

*(A cacophony of urban sound intensifies. All noise, except the droning of distant cars, ceases. **MARGARET**'s on her phone.)*

ISAAC. Beautiful.

MARGARET. Yeah.

ISAAC. Do you wanna –

MARGARET. You're taking up the blanket.

ISAAC. Oh. Sorry.

MARGARET. You're good.

(Pause.)

ISAAC. Do you wanna name one?

MARGARET. Name what?

ISAAC. A star.

MARGARET. Why would we do that.

ISAAC. I don't know. It's romantic?

I like your rings.

(Brutal pause.)

Margaret?

MARGARET. Yeah.

ISAAC. I thought you wanted to hangout and stuff.

MARGARET. Hangout.

ISAAC. Yes.

MARGARET. And stuff.

ISAAC. Yes.

MARGARET. So you just wanted to hook up with me and leave then.

ISAAC. I'm not following.

MARGARET. Dude. The blanket? The arm-around-the-shoulder thing? It's kinda obvious.

ISAAC. I just wanted to –

MARGARET. What? You wanted to what, Isaac?

ISAAC. TALK TO YOU?

Maybe?

(Pause.)

MARGARET. Shit. Sorry. God, I'm sorry.

I used to be so good at this.

ISAAC. What do you mean?

MARGARET. Just like, being with people?

I should go.

ISAAC. Hey, don't. I'm good. This is good.

MARGARET. Okay.

(Pause.)

Woah.

ISAAC. You good?

MARGARET. Yeah. Oh, yeah. I was just having a moment.

ISAAC. A moment.

MARGARET. Yeah. Like a spiritual thing.

ISAAC. What specifically –

MARGARET. The highway. Listen.

(They close their eyes, intently.)

It sorta...

ISAAC. Swallows you.

MARGARET. Damn.

(Pause.)

I was gonna say *enthralls*. Or *consumes*, but –

ISAAC. How's Audrey?

MARGARET. She's okay. Completely passed out after the party.

ISAAC. That sounds like her.

MARGARET. Really.

That vodka.

ISAAC. Yeah.

MARGARET. I mean we get wasted in OC but you Oakland people like *get wasted*.

ISAAC. I've never been into that kinda –

MARGARET. We should play a questions game. Oh my God we totally should.

ISAAC. Uh...

MARGARET. Me first.

How many girls have you been with?

ISAAC. What?

MARGARET. How many women have you –

ISAAC. No.

MARGARET. Isaac.

ISAAC. That's not fair.

MARGARET. You're required by law to answer.

ISAAC. What law?

MARGARET. My law. The law of the...questions game.

ISAAC. That's totally unethical.

MARGARET. Unethical un-shmethical.

(*Pause.*)

Fine. What's your favorite movie I guess.

ISAAC. You're gonna laugh.

MARGARET. No I won't.

ISAAC. You will.

MARGARET. Dude, literally –

(**MARGARET** *holds out her pinkie.* **ISAAC** *takes it reluctantly.*)

ISAAC. *The Notebook.*

(**MARGARET** *puts a hand over her mouth.*)

You're laughing.

MARGARET. I'm not.

ISAAC. Stop. It's a rad movie.

MARGARET. (*Laughing.*) Rad. It's so rad.

ISAAC. My turn.

MARGARET. Make it a juicy one.

ISAAC. Fine.

Are you into astrology?

(*Pause.*)

MARGARET. I'm a Libra.

ISAAC. Nice. I'm a Sag.

MARGARET. What?

ISAAC. I'm a Sagittarius.

MARGARET. Get out.

ISAAC. It's on my birth chart and everything.

MARGARET. You're actually into astrology.

ISAAC. It's more of a girl thing, huh?

MARGARET. Maybe.

I mean it's obviously all bullshit but we are the less intellectual sex.

(Pause.)

Kidding.

ISAAC. It's interesting that you're a Libra.

MARGARET. Oh?

ISAAC. You're all very – I don't know – sensitive? In the best way.

MARGARET. Thanks.

We're compatible, you know. *Astrologically*.

ISAAC. Oh. Cool. This is nice.

MARGARET. Totally.

Do you believe in God?

ISAAC. I go to church.

MARGARET. But do you believe in God.

ISAAC. I'm just so logical about it all.

Like, you either believe in a god that doesn't exist or you believe in a god that didn't stop the opioid epidemic. Or cure cancer. Or –

MARGARET. I believe in God.

ISAAC. You do?

MARGARET. But I don't *trust* God.

ISAAC. Explain.

(Pause.)

MARGARET. Wanna sneak out? God. Wanna get drunk? God. Wanna hookup? God.

Wanna get an abortion?

(Pause.)

God.

(She composes herself.)

Are you high?

ISAAC. What?

MARGARET. Are you on drugs?

ISAAC. Why are you asking me that?

MARGARET. I was just wondering if –

ISAAC. I'm not.

MARGARET. You seem nervous.

ISAAC. I'm not.

MARGARET. It's not that big of a deal.

ISAAC. I DON'T DO DRUGS.

MARGARET. Okay.

(Pause.)

ISAAC. I don't know why I'm here.

MARGARET. In this park?

ISAAC. No – why are we here right now?

MARGARET. That's a pretty big question, pal.

ISAAC. Why'd you come to Oakland?

MARGARET. To visit Audrey.

ISAAC. You guys aren't even that close.

MARGARET. We do live 500 miles away.

ISAAC. You're from Orange County.

MARGARET. So?

ISAAC. Disneyland's in Orange County.

MARGARET. What the hell does that have to do with anything.

ISAAC. Why not stay in Disneyland?

(Pause.)

MARGARET. Disneyland's not that great.

People don't really see me there.

I mean, they see me but they don't get me. They don't get why I do the things I do.

It's just boring. And boring is...

Well, it makes me sad.

ISAAC. You're not boring.

MARGARET. No. No I am not.

Do you like rock?

ISAAC. That's your question?

MARGARET. I asked, didn't I?

ISAAC. I'm not a fan.

MARGARET. Really.

ISAAC. It's loud.

MARGARET. What's wrong with loud?

ISAAC. I like quieter stuff. Older, I guess. Nina Simone, Chet Baker. I love that time period. I mean obviously life was a billion times worse back then but I don't know. Things were simpler?

Like, there's this scene in *The Notebook* where Rachel McAdams and whatever-his-name-is run into the street and this song by Billie Holiday starts playing. And they just dance.

And you think... *Wow*. They're really in love.

You never see that anymore. You never see two people in love actually dancing together. Like at homecoming there's always that one couple that's basically *flailing* and then a minute later they're hooking up in the bathroom. It's like...soulless.

Dancing is love. It's supposed to be love, right?

*(Sweet pause. **MARGARET** opens her phone.)*

MARGARET. Screw it.

*(**MARGARET** clicks play and a jazz standard plays[*].)*

ISAAC. What are you doing?

*(**MARGARET** stands.)*

MARGARET. We're gonna dance.

ISAAC. Margaret –

---

[*] A license to produce *Oakland* does not include a performance license for any third-party or copyrighted music. Licensees should create an original composition or use music in the public domain. For further information, please see the Music and Third Party Materials Use Note on page iii.

(MARGARET *begins to sway. After a moment, she takes* ISAAC's *hand.* ISAAC *pulls away. Pause.*)

MARGARET. When I had the, um…

I didn't think they would react the way they did. I didn't –

ISAAC. Margaret.

(*Pause.*)

You're not boring.

MARGARET. You already said that.

ISAAC. You're like the least boring person I've ever met.

(*Pause.*)

MARGARET. Isaac?

ISAAC. Yeah.

MARGARET. Let's listen to something else.

(*Music stops. The cacophony of urban noise swells, engulfing* MARGARET *and* ISAAC.)

End

REVERIE

Jacqueline Vellandi

REVERIE was first produced at the International Thespian Festival over Zoom on June 25, 2021. The performance was directed by William Myatt with dramaturgical work by Mark Kaufmann. The production stage manager was Matthew Genchev. The cast was as follows:

SHANE	Jeron Robinson
ALEX	Olivia Garland
DYLAN	Diego Sanchez-Galvan
TEACHER 1	Alex Irwin
TEACHER 2	Regan Bobich
TEACHER 3	Abby Shamrell

CHARACTERS

SHANE
ALEX
DYLAN
TEACHER 1
TEACHER 2
TEACHER 3

SETTING

In a classroom and later in a reverie as big or as small as the director's imagination.

TIME

Any time past, present, or future when we've just needed to sit back and press pause on reality.

AUTHOR'S NOTES

The pronouns used throughout the script are representative of the original cast, but they may be replaced as necessary. All names were chosen to be unisex. Any character can be played by any race or gender because this tale is a universal story.

Scene One

*(Three chairs and three respective desks sit on stage. A school bell rings. Three students, **SHANE**, **ALEX**, and **DYLAN** enter from three different spots. These three can be played by any gender, changing pronouns as necessary. They hurry across the stage, each walking an elaborate route while holding a conversation with an invisible being.)*

SHANE. Babe I don't know what to tell you. I can't hang out.

ALEX. What did you get for question three again?

DYLAN. My mom is gonna kill me.

SHANE. I know. I'm sorry. I'm just really busy.

ALEX. Really? That's not even close to what I got.

DYLAN. Maybe I can make it up somehow, you know?

SHANE. Maybe next week, okay?

ALEX. How did you get that?

DYLAN. I am so dead.

*(The students make their way to their respective seats and sit with a thud. They drop their textbooks onto the desk at the same time. **TEACHERS 1, 2,** and **3** enter and stand behind the three students.)*

TEACHERS. Good morning class.

SHANE. I pledge allegiance to the flag

ALEX. of the United States of America,

DYLAN. and to the republic for which it stands,

SHANE. one Nation under God, indivisible,

ALEX. with liberty

DYLAN. and justice

SHANE, ALEX & DYLAN. for all.

TEACHER 1. Open your textbook to page 72.

TEACHER 2. page 126.

TEACHER 3. page 394.

> (**SHANE, ALEX,** *and* **DYLAN** *open their textbooks simultaneously to a random page.*)

TEACHER 1. This first industrial revolution came at a time when...

TEACHER 2. X is equal to negative b, plus or minus the square root of...

TEACHER 3. Remember to annotate every time the author uses the color yellow as a description for...

> (**SHANE, ALEX,** *and* **DYLAN** *rest their heads on their text books. The* **TEACHERS** *exit slowly.*)

Scene Two

(The students lift their heads one at a time.)

SHANE. Does anyone actually pay attention to that class?

ALEX. I had her last year. I don't think anyone pays attention.

SHANE. I needed this break.

ALEX. Right? Same.

> *(**DYLAN** crumples up a piece of paper and throws it offstage. He gets up out of his seat, picks up the textbook upside down and walks downstage.)*

DYLAN. Guys come here real fast.

> *(**SHANE** and **ALEX** come to stand on either side of **DYLAN**. They all read the upside down textbook.)*

Check this out.

SHANE. What are we looking at?

ALEX. Dylan you're holding it upside down.

DYLAN. You don't see it?

SHANE. See what?

DYLAN. Look. Right here is my little cottage.

> *(**DYLAN** points to a spot on the page. Then, to another spot.)*

And here is –

ALEX. – My townhouse!

SHANE. What?

ALEX. You don't see it?

SHANE. It's upside down.

ALEX. Look Shane, it's right there.

(**ALEX** *points to a spot on the page.*)

SHANE. Is that...is that my fishing hut? It is!

DYLAN. What's this right here?

(**DYLAN** *points to a spot on the page.*)

SHANE. Isn't that the...

ALEX. The orange trees! Can't you smell them?

(**ALEX** *stands up to smell them.*)

DYLAN. When I was younger, my mom would pack an orange in my lunch every day. And when she came to wake me up, her hands would smell like oranges. It happened every day. Soon her hands stopped smelling like oranges and instead, oranges started smelling like her hands.

(**SHANE** *goes back to his desk and sits on it.*)

SHANE. If you need me, I'll be fishing right outside my hut.

(**SHANE** *mimics casting a line, waiting, then eventually reeling it in and repeating the process.*)

My dad used to take me out on a kayak to go fishing all the time. We would sit there on the water as the sun came up and laugh with each other for hours... I don't think we ever caught anything.

DYLAN. Sure is a nice day out.

ALEX. It is, isn't it? I think I'll go for a hike. My sister would have loved it here. She used to go hiking all the time. I wish I would've gone with her more, but I was always just so busy.

(**ALEX** *begins to "hike" around the stage.*)

DYLAN. I smell the oranges.

ALEX. Feel that nice breeze?

DYLAN. The water is so blue.

(**DYLAN** *takes in this world for a beat. He's in love.*)

I think I'll go for a swim.

(**DYLAN** *lays on his desk and mimics swimming.* **ALEX**'s *route has led her back to her desk. She climbs onto the chair, and then the desk. She stands, looks out, and throws her arms open.*)

ALEX. I'm the king of the world!

(**DYLAN** *begins to struggle.*)

DYLAN. The current's so strong!

(**SHANE** *reels in his line and hurries towards* **DYLAN**.)

SHANE. Come on, get out!

DYLAN. It's pulling me under!

ALEX. What?

DYLAN. Help! Help!

(**ALEX** *turns around and "hikes" back to* **DYLAN** *and* **SHANE**. **DYLAN** *is laying motionless on the ground.* **SHANE** *grabs his hands and drags him a bit.*)

ALEX. Is he...?

(**DYLAN** *begins to cough. He rolls over onto his stomach and the coughing turns into laughing.*)

ALEX. Stop laughing! You scared us!

DYLAN. I'm sorry.

ALEX. I'd finally made it to the top! And then I had to come all the way back down for you.

(SHANE helps DYLAN up.)

DYLAN. *(To ALEX.)* I'm sorry I scared you. Are you going to go back up to the top of the mountain?

ALEX. *(Shrugs.)* Probably not. I made it to the top; I just wish I'd gotten to enjoy it a little more.

SHANE. What time do you think it is?

ALEX. How would I know?

(Silence. No one knows quite what to do.)

SHANE. I'm bored.

ALEX. Then go back.

DYLAN. Don't go back!

SHANE. Why not? Is it really that bad?

DYLAN. Yes…isn't it?

SHANE. I'm not sure.

ALEX. We never remember how bad it is.

SHANE. Maybe we never remember how good it is.

DYLAN. If we go back, we won't remember how good *this* is.

SHANE. This isn't good. It's boring.

DYLAN. We can just breathe. In and out. Smell the oranges.

SHANE. The smell of oranges makes me a sick after a while.

DYLAN. We can go fishing!

ALEX. What's the point? We'll never catch anything.

DYLAN. And we can hike to the top of the mountain!

SHANE. Been there, done that.

DYLAN. Come on guys! We can do anything here!

ALEX. I don't want to do anything right now.

DYLAN. So then...now what?

(Beat.)

ALEX. Now we go back.

DYLAN. There's nothing to go back to. This is it. This is our whole lives.

ALEX. It can't be our whole lives. There was something before...wasn't there?

SHANE. It does kind of feel like we've been here forever.

ALEX. That doesn't mean we were, though. Come on. Don't either of you remember anything?

SHANE. Yeah I remember.

DYLAN. You do?

SHANE. Sure. When we go back, we'll never have to guess what to do next. Everywhere we look people are telling us what to do. Every minute, every second is filled.

DYLAN. That sounds horrible.

ALEX. No it doesn't. Imagine never getting bored and always knowing the next step to take.

DYLAN. But other people choose the next step for you. I wanna stay here.

SHANE. We're frozen here Dylan. We need to go back to where time actually moves.

ALEX. Dylan?

DYLAN. I have a feeling I don't have a choice.

> *(Beat. All resolved to go back, they stand realizing they don't know how to go back.)*

ALEX. So...

SHANE. Maybe it's just giving us time to say goodbye.

ALEX. I guess one last hike can't hurt.

> *(**ALEX** begins to "hike" around the space.)*

DYLAN. What do you say Shane? Wanna go fishing?

SHANE. I've never caught anything.

DYLAN. Maybe this will be the time you do.

> *(**SHANE** sits on his desk and "casts a line." **DYLAN** takes a breath and goes to his desk for a "swim.")*

ALEX. Goodbye mountain.

SHANE. Goodbye river.

DYLAN. Goodbye orange trees.

> *(They sigh, taking in the peace. **DYLAN** notices the textbook sitting face down. He walks over to it. He turns it over and studies it.)*

Who messed up the map?

ALEX. What do you mean?

DYLAN. Come here.

> *(**ALEX** turns around and hikes back. **DYLAN** holds it right side up and shows it to **ALEX**.)*

Look. Our houses are gone.

ALEX. So is the river and the mountain.

DYLAN. What is all this?

ALEX. Shane you should really come look at this.

SHANE. No way! Just so he can try to convince us not to go back.

> (**DYLAN** *sits in his seat and studies the textbook.*)

DYLAN. The 1918 influenza pandemic was unusually deadly and caused by the H1N1 Influenza A virus –

SHANE. Read in your head. I'm trying to catch a fish.

DYLAN. It lasted from February 1918 to April 1920.

SHANE. I don't want to hear about this. I want to go back!

DYLAN. It infected 500 million people.

> (**SHANE** *sits in his seat and lays his head on the table with his hands covering his ears.*)

SHANE. La la la la la la la.

> (**SHANE** *continues to make noise, trying to drown out* **DYLAN**'s *reading.*)

DYLAN. It infected about a third of the world's population at the time. It had four successive waves.

> (*Intrigued,* **ALEX** *returns to her desk.*)

ALEX. I think it's working.

DYLAN. The forgotten pandemic. It was overshadowed by the destruction of World War I. World War I. A global war originating in Europe that lasted from 1914 to 1918. Twenty million deaths and twenty-one million wounded. It's just a history book, but I don't want to go back to this.

ALEX. It's not just a history book Dylan. Don't you get it? That's the whole lesson right there. That's the real world.

*(**ALEX** buries her head in her hands. **DYLAN**, too, is tired of reading and slams the book shut on his desk. This startles all three to sit up.)*

Scene Three

(They stare blankly ahead. The **THREE TEACHERS** *re-enter and stand behind their respective students.)*

TEACHER 3. For homework tonight you will write about the effects of the Spanish influenza.

TEACHER 2. And do problems 3-27 through 4-21 in your book.

TEACHER 1. And don't forget to read the next two chapters by yourself.

TEACHER 3. I will also be collecting your analysis on the relationship between the 1918 pandemic and the First World War, so we can work on our SAQs next class.

TEACHER 2. Make sure you show all your work for every problem. I'll be checking, and if you don't have clear work and circled answers, you will not be getting credit.

TEACHER 1. Once you finish the book, we'll jump into the rough drafts of your essays. Remember to refer to your notes from our Socratic Seminar as much as possible.

TEACHER 3. It should only take an hour or so if you work diligently.

TEACHER 2. The homework in this class won't take more than an hour if you don't take any breaks.

TEACHER 1. I know it will take a couple hours, but I haven't given too much homework recently. So, you can do it.

TEACHERS 1, 2 & 3. Be ready to turn it in next class. Have a good weekend guys.

SHANE, ALEX & DYLAN. Thank you.

(The **TEACHERS** *exit.* **SHANE** *and* **ALEX** *stand up.)*

SHANE. I know, I know, I'm sorry. I have a lot of work to catch up on. Next week though I promise we'll hang out.

ALEX. I'm freaking out. I totally zoned out and missed the whole lesson, and now I have no clue how to do any of it.

> *(***SHANE*** and* **ALEX** *exit.* **DYLAN** *sits alone, still staring blankly ahead.* **DYLAN** *takes a deep breath, then opens the textbook and begins to read.)*

End